International Negotiation

International Negotiation

A Cross-Cultural Perspective

Glen Fisher

Intercultural Press Inc.

ISBN: 0-933662-24-6

Library of Congress No.: 81-85716

Note: This is a revised version of a discussion paper first prepared for the Foreign Service Institute, Department of State, to support training activities. It is not a statement of policy nor of official position.

TABLE OF CONTENTS

INTRODUCTION

This work tries to address an often under-appreciated facet of international negotiation: the cross-cultural communication process that is involved whenever persons of widely differing backgrounds attempt to reach agreements. The central problem is that while one may recognize that negotiating internationally does pose a task in coping with a wider range of styles of decision-making, perception of objectives, or thought processes than would be encountered at home, "cultural factors" is a vague and fuzzy concept not easily translated into practical application. We will attempt to demonstrate this cross-cultural reality in international negotiation with Japanese, Mexican and French counterparts and suggest a line of questioning and analysis that a negotiator might find useful whatever the national identity.

A cross-cultural dimension is recognized, in effect, in simply anticipating that there will probably be something "foreign" in doing business even with German or Canadian counterparts, whose cultures and world views are much like an American's, and in expecting that almost certainly there will be something to take into account when cultural contrasts are more pronounced. Potential for misunderstanding will be greater; more time will be lost in talking past each other. More complete explanations of positions may be needed or a special kind of persuasive skill called for. It is naive indeed to venture into international negotiation with the untempered self assurance that "after all, people are pretty much alike everywhere." The best experience in domestic situations may not go far abroad.

The cultural difference that has to be taken into account may turn out to be as important as that found in certain contrasting sets of values that determine the hierarchy of negotiating objectives themselves, or as trivial as behavior mannerisms that subtly block confidence and trust. Even gestures and other non-verbal behavior may contribute to a psychological unease that makes communication more difficult. Differing forms of social amenities or notions of status and dignity can throw personal egos off balance. All these factors make an impact even before the substance of negotiation is addressed.

Sometimes such complications exist even when cosmopolitan experience on both sides or similar cultural background would seem to reduce the difficulty. In such situations small but real differences are less easily recognized and taken into consideration. And cultural factors can be significant in varying degrees in a range from the most formal negotiations to the most routine where the bulk of negotiation actually takes place. Thus, across the board, these matters require studied attention as one tries to capture the logic and intent of the other side or tries to be persuasive or assure that one's own position is understood without misperception and distortion.

It is recognized that in some international work cultural factors are less relevant. Obviously, the modern intensity of international interaction, especially in business and in technological, communication and educational fields, has produced something of an internationalized "culture" which reduces the clash of cultural background and stereotyped images. Happily for us this **modus vivendi** is largely based on Western practices and even on the English language, so many otherwise "foreign" counterparts are accommodating to the American style of negotiation.

Still, much routine negotiation takes place in less cosmopolitan contexts, and often by people in highly specialized fields who are called upon to conduct international negotiations of some kind without a background of sustained foreign experience. Scientists, technical experts, or air transport regulators would be examples, with their problems compounded as they may have to work intensely but only briefly in a series of different countries and cultures. Further, by the nature of their assignments they may have to deal with specialized counterparts who also have limited international experience.

Even in diplomatic practice, negotiation is not necessarily confined to formal talks looking toward written and signed agreements or treaties. It also takes place routinely when an Embassy officer calls at the foreign office to urge, for example, a supportive position on a UN issue as per Department instruction. Or negotiation may involve the way a local tax law is to be applied, seeking assistance in staging a cultural event, getting a shipment out of customs, or renting office space. A consular section's protection and welfare officer faces a constant round of frequently ambiguous situations in which cooperation is sought from officials whose outlooks often are narrowly those of the local society. And even when formal negotiations are concerned, long hours are spent in preparatory work at levels where perceptions and reactions are more likely to be culture-bound.

This paper is based on a project carried out for the Department of State's Foreign Service Institute to support training activities, but is being published for its more general applicability to a wide range of professionals who work internationally: business executives, educators, scientists, technical assistance specialists, volunteer agency personnel, reporters and those who manage the linkage of an increasing variety of trans-national organizations and institutions. In order to reflect actual experience, it was decided at the start to choose three countries which would present differing kinds of negotiating problems, and then by comparatively exploring bi-lateral negotiation dynamics in that context, establish a range of factors which comprise a cultural dimension in any negotiation. The choice of Japan, Mexico and France was rather arbitrary. This will not, therefore, be a definitive discussion of how to negotiate specifically with the Japanese, Mexicans or French. Rather these cases are intended to supply illustrations—hopefully with reasonable accuracy— to support an important direction of inquiry. It is this direction of inquiry itself that is proposed as the practical objective for most readers whose concerns will be related to negotiations with other national and cultural groups.

To sample real experience, interview discussions were conducted with some thirty Foreign Service officers who had lived, specialized in, or conducted negotiations in one or more of these countries. The substance of such negotiation typically involved cooperative projects or commercial, military, administrative or regulatory problems. Various source materials were also used. The most important are footnoted.

The way all this has been done, however, reflects my own specialization in analyzing psychological and cultural factors in foreign affairs and international communication processes. My perspective is that of a former Foreign Service Officer who, perhaps uniquely, had an academic and research background in cultural anthropology and sociology. Along with conventional Departmental and overseas assignments, I served as Dean of the Foreign Service Institute's School of Area Studies and pursued further study of the psycho-cultural dimension of international relations during an assignment at Tuft University's Fletcher School of Law and Diplomacy.

NEGOTIATIONS, CULTURE
AND SOCIAL PSYCHOLOGY

By its nature the negotiation process is a study in social psychology. It proceeds, after all, as an interplay of perception, information processing, and reaction, all of which turn on images of reality (accurate or not), on implicit assumptions regarding the issue being negotiated, and on an underlying matrix of conventional wisdom, beliefs, and social expectations. This becomes more apparent when the negotiation process is international, for these matters are functions of culture. They tend to attract little attention when the players share the same cultural base, but they surface quickly when the differing psychological predispositions of two cultures meet.

Domestically, study of negotiation typically tends to be focussed on all that goes on between the parties—the tactics and ploys, bargaining strategy, use of supporting data, equating of interests, fall-back positions, etc. In its extreme this approach is sometimes reduced to game theory exercises in which the negotiators themselves seem to be almost interchangeable. And in part, they may be, for despite individual qualities, they share a familiarity with the same society and culture. When the players have been socialized in different cultures, however, they are much less interchangeable. Consequently, more specific attention has to be given to what goes on **inside** the heads of negotiators on both sides of the table as they perceive the interests and issues at hand and choose their responses. Beyond the **individual** variations in this regard which practiced negotiators normally fully appreciate, there will be variations in patterns of psychological behavior that go with shared culture. For this reason games and simulations applied to international negotiation often fall apart.

In practical application defining instances of significant cultural contrast might be subject to some debate, depending on the problem at hand. It could be argued that corporation managers or diplomats would share more professional culture with their international counterparts than these same groups would share within their own societies with college professors or factory workers. However, for the purposes of the present exercise, we are first concerned with culture in terms of national societies.

All this may appear formidably technical, but it is basic. The negotiator needs to capture some of the social psychologist's perspective even though the more technical aspects of psychology necessarily are left to the professionals in that field. It is one of those cases where psychology is too important to be left to the psychologists.

It is worth noting that in making calculations in international affairs there is a growing precedent for using cultural and psychological approaches. Some interest has developed in relation to management and corporate-level negotiation, but the most extensive inquiry has been directed toward inter-governmental relations. For example, John Stoessinger in his **Nations in Darkness** makes a strong case in illustrating how pervasive misperceptions have been in the most important positions taken by the U.S., Russia and China in their relations with each other. These instances range from American assumptions about Chiang Kai-shek's qualities of leadership and pro-Americanism to Russian assumptions regarding American docility in the Cuban missile crisis.[1] Yale psychologist Irving Janis, in his book with the provocative title **Victims of Groupthink**, shows how the collective unexamined assumptions of policy-makers get reinforced in group processes that go with decision-making.[2] Robert Jervis has made a notable impact on scholarly analysis in the international relations field with his recent **Perception and Misperception in International Politics**. Jervis suggests that not only should would-be experts consider this dimension, but they should also become much more qualified in using basic psychological approaches and tools.[3] The Cyprus dispute and, of course, the Arab-Israeli confrontation have lent themselves to a variety of psycho-cultural studies.

Stanford University's Alexander George stresses the need to consider how psychological processes affect the quality of reasoning in his **Presidential Decisionmaking in Foreign Policy: The Effective Use of Information and Advice.**[4] He sees the course of international relations as partly a function of how leaders use the information available to them in the light of their existing beliefs and images, and partly a result of their ability as problem-solvers to objectively program their mental processes to establish the context and meaning of new events or to try to understand an opponent's perspective.

Hopefully, the reader will find the psycho-cultural approach coming into sharper focus as comparative examples help flesh out the categories of culturally related problems set forth in the following sections of this study. But the stage might be better set by noting briefly how some of the normal features of thought and perception become booby traps in communication when two or more cultures are involved.

First, especially as applied to negotiation, human minds are **information processors** and can be understood by the way they receive, store, organize and use information. But while people are born with this capacity, just how an adult mind does this depends on how it turns out to be programmed. The mind has to, in effect, get itself organized in order to provide some kind of system by which remembered information and experience can be applied to cope with subsequent exposure to still more experience and information. Thus, mental constructs of the external world, beliefs, images, implicit assumptions, and habits of reasoning develop so that new stimuli and even fragmentary perceptions can be taken in and given meaning without a continuous groping process. For example, one can judge a table top to be rectangular even though no right angles strike the retina of the eye, or one can see a price on a gas pump and think: energy shortage. A passage of music might trigger an image of a German composer; a signature on a contract will set off a pattern of expectations regarding how to comply with the agreement's terms.

The problem is that communication depends on there being a reasonable similarity of such programming between the communicators. But as culture supplies the master programming to a very large extent, such a similarity cannot be relied on when cultures differ. And in general the more abstract the subject, the more probable it will be that the basics will differ by culture.

Secondly, it follows that our perception habits become locked in to a much greater degree than we imagine—so much so that in both physical and social perception it may be almost impossible to "see" something that conflicts with the way we expect to see it. Hence, we are subject to optical illusions, or let stereotypes flaw our judgements. The fundamental idea here is that in order to be minimally efficient, a certain **internal consistency** among our beliefs, images, information constructs, etc., develops in the normal process of learning and maturing. Then, because the mind resists having this consistency disturbed, we attempt to perceive in a way that makes new stimuli or information fit into our existing organization of ideas and beliefs, or we tend to reject or seek consistent explanations for new information that does not mesh congenially. Negotiating internationally almost certainly means having to cope with new and inconsistent information, usually accompanied by new behavior, social environments, even sights and smells. One can override some of these unconscious habits of mind, but that is not automatic even when the signals indicate there is a problem. An intellectual effort of a different order is required which depends on a conscious analysis of alternative explanations, and even on an attempt to capture some notion of the pattern of internal consistency supplied by a counterpart's culture.

As a third point, note that the naive normal outlook is to assume that the implicit assumptions and habitual ways of thinking of one's own society are a matter of human nature or that they have universal application—or should have. Consequently, in cross-cultural situations, confusion turns full circle when the mind not only places its own stamp of meaning on an incoming message, but goes further to **project** that same meaning to the other party. It may seem a long step to go from the projection theory set forth in a sophomore psychology course to applications in world affairs, but it is clear that it applies. For example, Marc Lewis documented this tendency in Central Intelligence Agency estimates written on Viet Nam. He found that the analysts interpreted developments by projecting much more of an American frame of reference onto events than they were aware. This led to serious distortions of meaning and of implication when they tried to explain the "foreign" happenings in Vietnamese society and culture. He titled his report "The Blind Spot of U.S. Foreign Intelligence."[5]

Fourth, one form of unconscious projection that wreaks particular havoc on negotiation is **attribution of motive**. The idea here, as treated in various forms of attribution theory in social psychology, is that people normally and constantly attribute motives to others with whom they interact, whether they are conscious that they are doing so or not.[6] The motives attributed are, of course, those common to one's normal experience with people in general and with the person in question, or at least that category of person, along with one's definition of the situation of the moment. Such attribution as, "naturally, he wants to make a profit," or, "he is hesitating because he has not understood what I said," might be samples of assumed motives that hardly need to be thought through to get on with an exchange taking place in one's own culture. There the chances of being correct in assuming motives are relatively high. Chances diminish quickly, however, when a cross-cultural situation is encountered, and decline even more when the subject at issue is abstract and complex. This reality is familiar enough in the foreign service or in corporate public relations abroad; it seems that others are constantly misattributing our motives either naively or perversely. But in our own ethnocentrism it is much less recognizable that we too misattribute motives. Combine the error on both sides and it can be argued that nothing obstructs international negotiation so much as this natural psychological mechanism running amok in a cross-cultural situation.

Without going further in this sketchy overview of the social psychology of cross-cultural communication, let us turn to more concrete applications.

FIRST CONSIDERATION:
THE PLAYERS AND THE SITUATION

To begin demonstrating psycho-cultural factors in negotiation, one starts logically with the social interaction process itself. As an American's conception of a dinner party differs from that of a Japanese or a Frenchman, so do preconceptions regarding a negotiating session. Images held differ in such subtle aspects as a session's social meaning, who should attend, what kind of conversations should take place, with what courtesy, and with what expected style of debate. **It is apparent that there can be a cultural dimension in the way that negotiators view the negotiation encounter itself.**

Starting with the Japanese case: Westerners who negotiate with Japanese feel that the whole idea of holding a formal session specifically to negotiate is somewhat foreign to many Japanese. Americans are frustrated when their counterparts do not enter into an expected give-and-take, and some argue in frustration that it is time for the Japanese to learn to adapt to more internationalized conventions of negotiation. The frustration is greater, it might be added, when the Japanese seem to win at least their share of negotiating points.

The cross-cultural factors here are not hard to locate. There is little in Japanese culture to make Japanese feel comfortable with articulate advocacy in polite company, most especially in formal settings. They see such as the occasion to ceremonially adopt what has already been worked out in a patient consensus-generating process. To openly disagree at a formal stage is distasteful and embarrassing, like enduring a husband and wife spat at our above-mentioned dinner party. Certainly the Japanese are not prepared to change their position in such a setting. Not only

17

would this be bad taste, but it would conflict with their decision-making process, as will be discussed later. Nor is it easy for them to tolerate the surprises that are normally a part of adversary proceedings. One officer recalled his acute embarrassment when, after carefully going over the text of his ambassador's speech in advance with his Japanese counterparts precisely to provide a smooth no-surprises session, the ambassador on the spur of the moment discarded the speech and spoke extemporaneously. The substance was not changed, but the credibility of the working level officer was set back severely.

Harmony is important to Japanese. They still use go-betweens to assure smoothness in social relations in all kinds of dealings from arranging weddings to making political accommodations. One officer noted that such a role was played by his Yokohama landlord's daughter in far-away Seattle simply in the course of selling him his refrigerator (but not the stove, as it turned out) when he departed. In fact, this emphasis on smooth relations in public exists in many societies; it is frequently reported from Thailand and Indonesia.

On the other hand, the American's view of a negotiating encounter is influenced by a very different culture base, one in which efficient conduct of business is what life is all about, where people gain prestige by being persuasive in public forums, where tactics in maneuvering a debate are accepted, where it is assumed that one probably will have to give in a bit, pragmatically, to gain a compromise—which itself is a most honorable result. Americans do expect to probe for the other side's fallback position. But they like a straightforward approach. One observer suggested that Americans are more likely to start out expecting to trust the other party until proven untrustworthy, while the French, for instance, would be inclined to mistrust until good faith is proven.

Most of all, Americans see negotiating sessions as **problem-solving exercises**, and "problems" are precisely the dragons that Americans take joy in slaying. In the State

Department, I recall officers accusing a Country Director of being prepared to create crises when none existed because he so enjoyed meeting crises. Hardly a Japanese outlook!

Hence, as seen among our sample countries, negotiation difficulties sometimes arise because there is a difference in what negotiators **expect** of a negotiation's social setting, even though negotiators are often chosen in the first place for their experience in dealing with Americans. French expectations would, in any event, be similar to American. They would have no difficulty with advocacy and open disagreement, and in routine negotiation they seem to be relatively pragmatic in working toward problem-solving. But still their sense of the situation differs. To them, negotiation is an established art with long tradition in international diplomatic and business relations, with French negotiators and the French language at center stage. Thus they reflect a sense of self-assurance as they present the logic of their position. They do not see the negotiating table quite so much as a place for bargaining as one for searching out the reasoned solutions for which they have so carefully prepared. To them, the negotiation setting becomes more of a debating forum, with flexibility and accommodation simply for the sake of agreement less of an expectation.

How important is form, hospitality and protocol? Americans tend to downplay it. Certainly the French carry with them somewhat more of a sense of the formal and of proper hospitality. French government representatives encounter little dissent from their tax-payers when they provide appropriate dinners and receptions to go along with the occasion, even in low level negotiations. In contrast, note that Americans serving abroad unhappily have to suffer a citizenry that is suspicious of governmental representation accounts and too much expenditure for pomp and circumstance. Therefore, American delegations often look to co-operating American private groups or companies to bear the cost of receptions as their own Congress sees such as relatively unessential to negotiation. Even President Carter had to sell places at the White House banquet honoring the

Israeli-Egyptian peace signing—undoubtedly rather crude by French standards, and even astonishing to the Japanese with their expense-account culture.

The very function of entertainment and social activity related to negotiation can vary markedly by cultural norms. Americans comfortably **use** relaxed social occasions to conduct business; to others this might feel awkward, a breach of etiquette, particularly if the American is the guest.

The Mexican sense of the negotiation encounter seems to range widely, depending on the issue and the occasion, and to differ when negotiating with the United States as compared with other countries. When not dealing with Americans, the sense of formal social occasion and protocol is stronger. There is little satisfaction in Mexican tradition in getting down to business to solve problems in public forums. On the contrary, a value on form and ceremony goes back through Spanish heritage. This is gentlemanly and elite ground. Rhetoric and the grand idea are pursued. It is a time for distinguished performance, and a time to demonstrate ideal conceptions of Mexican civilization. It is not a time for objective analysis and pragmatic application.

Much of this preference for formal occasion carries over in dealing with Americans, but with resigned recognition that with the Americans being who and what they are, the discussion will, in fact, get down to practical business. Still, Mexicans see little virtue in a frank exchange, and they are concerned that negotiation to the north is always a testing time for Mexican honor. They like to see themselves as more reserved, able to maintain dignity, not like the Americans, who, they say, are like frogs—every time they open their mouths they expose everything inside.

It can be argued that the very idea of specifically scheduling an occasion to sit down and negotiate is Western. Those who come from a non-Western tradition have to learn to enter into the give-and-take of negotiation. In Indonesia, for example, it is reported that an effort is sometimes specifically made to train inexperienced Indonesians for participation in international conferences, that is, to prepare them for the intellectual confrontation that can be expected. Indonesians complain that they have no opportunity to talk "with the heart." Japanese often depend on the interaction of feelings for communication, sometimes as a substitute for intellectual exposition. They are comfortable with "belly talk."

Even when these contrasts are understood intellectually by both sides, latent uncomfortable feelings and tendencies to misattribute motives remain. The American may appear aggressive and rude; the Japanese standoffish and inscrutable. The Mexicans seem overly dramatic and impractical. The French are said to be the most "difficult" of Europeans—they spend their time making speeches and rationalizing without bargaining and compromising. From a cross-cultural perspective, a beautiful negotiating session is in the eye of the beholder!

Then there is the question: is there a national style in **choosing** negotiators? What kinds of people qualify to occupy the positions that call for conducting business with foreign counterparts? How are negotiating teams selected? When one tries to anticipate a counterpart's behavior, it is well to be able to go beyond the biographic data to understand that person's expected organizational or institutional role. In the case of negotiating teams, it is useful to know how their bureaucratic or business culture determines the members' relationships to each other. This sets the internal dynamics of the team.

For Americans, technical competence is basic. It is the **position** that supplies the authority for incumbents whose background is an egalitarian society. Only at higher levels of negotiation does the American negotiator tend to be selected on the basis of personal qualities of power or authority— perhaps as a representative of the president or as a recognized political or executive leader. Usually Americans find themselves selected to negotiate because they occupy a job that places them in that position, either to negotiate alone or in teams. In government teams they often primarily represent an agency and its view of the national interest rather than the country at large. They get their jobs and advance as professionals in specialties. Such factors as social background, age, the school they graduated from, and personal connections have relatively little to do with the fact that they are negotiators. The same is true of business negotiators. They judge themselves and each other by competence and success in large part and by the way they represent their firms or their sections of government. Their **social** egos are not particularly placed on the line, especially as compared with negotiators of many other countries.

A Japanese team presents more of a closed circle. Cultural conditioning that stresses orderliness in group dynamics rules the relationships among the members and defines their confrontation with the non-Japanese world. The progression to leadership and status is by professional competence, but also very much by seniority and experience. Hence, the team leader might be only marginally competent in the specific subject matter under negotiation, but still be the obvious head. He holds his position by being the representative of a consensus process through which the negotiating position has been derived. His technical command may depend on subordinates, but his symbolic authority is high. Age is important. His credentials for leadership are his survival through a highly competitive educational process that put him in the right university in the first place—typically Tokyo University if he ended up in the Foreign Office—and his network of colleagues who have moved up with him through the power structure on a parallel seniority basis. Thus members of Japanese teams honor a quite different mix of qualities in their professional and managerial careers than Americans.

The Mexican pattern is still different. Individuals on a negotiating team do stand out. The factors which bring them into a negotiating position are much more likely to reflect their personal qualities and social connections or leverage inside a political or business system in which personality counts in much greater degree than in the United States. Mexicans talk of an individual's prospects in terms of his "ubicación"—where he is "plugged in" in the system.

Personal relationships among team members—or lack of them—have much more to do with team dynamics. Leaders do see their social egos more on the line, and the culture tends to heighten sensitivity to violations of personal dignity. To judge the authority of a Mexican counterpart, it is therefore more important to explore his personal connections and the factions or special interest groups he represents—labor, government corporations, or whatever. For example, in one negotiation on air transport agreements a team included not only representatives of the airlines, but also of the pilots and ground personnel. It is reported that in some cases there can be as much of a challenge in arriving at positions that Mexican team members can agree on among themselves, as ones that both teams can accept. It is a system that makes preparatory work difficult for Mexicans and poses problems for Americans as formal negotiations proceed.

It may not always be apparent which Mexican team members hold personal authority. Sometimes power is signaled by the presence of a personal assistant or underling, possibly even one of the members of the negotiating team. This would be the man who carries the papers, defers to his patron, enlarges the presence of the weighty official.

French qualification to be a government negotiator takes on a uniqueness as the qualities and function of the French bureaucracy are reflected. Traditionally the French civil service has carried more prestige than the American and has been relied on to a much greater extent as the stable and responsible element of French government. French officialdom comes from a less egalitarian society than the American; its members reflect somewhat more assurance of social position. But this is not necessarily social connection as in the Mexican scene. It is more a social status qualification for entering a system that then stresses competence and adherence to standards. The typical senior officer might well have gone through the demanding French National School of Administration. The French system is one that prompts its negotiators to do their preparatory work carefully and with a practiced eye for managing political considerations and the interconnected interests of French ministeries and bureaus. The same set of criteria and values apply in the French corporate setting.

However the French counterpart's actual competence is judged, the chances are that he will enjoy a high degree of self-assurance in international negotiation because his system prepares him for it and backs him up. It gives him prestige and authority. Further, it supplies a certain tradition of French primacy in international relations—they have negotiated with "barbarians" for centuries. The French negotiator is not likely to feel inadequate to the task. One American negotiator remarked that the French have a highly sophisticated ability to make their opposites feel inadequate.

There is, then, a difference in professional self-image that American, Japanese, Mexican and French negotiators carry with them when social position, education and the use made of it, method of selection, and the way that influence is exercised in their own organizations are taken into account.

This helps define a problem that often plagues international negotiation: **conflicting expectations in role behavior—a particularly useful conceptual tool in cross-cultural analysis**. One can begin to sort out what is going on here by carefully observing the social and cultural environment of one's counterpart and asking what patterns of behavior are expected to go with being a corporate executive, diplomatic officer, bureau director, technical consultant, legal advisor or police chief in—for the illustrative purposes of this discussion—Japan, Mexico, or France. It is a line of inquiry that any negotiator can use to advantage. It asks both what the formal "job description" is and also what the less forthrightly stated but nonetheless binding subtleties are. These may range from specific attire or life style to the incumbent's sense of when deference is granted and when it is due.

It is this kind of preparatory questioning that helps tell you, if you find any answers, where your counterpart "is coming from"—to use today's jargon. While he may actually behave differently in international company than in his culture-bound office, it is highly useful to be able to anticipate who your counterpart thinks he is, what qualities he and his colleagues respect in someone occupying that position, how he expects to relate to other people in his organization, and so forth.

For example, in Mexico there is nothing to specifically tell you that an executive or office director is supposed to act in an authoritarian manner or even reflect a degree of **machismo**, but observation of those who are effective and esteemed as against those who are not will be suggestive. A Japanese job description may not specify Tokyo University, but a search for role qualifications might establish this expectation.

Role behavior is essentially what we have been discussing throughout this section, of course. Much of this is summed up in an approach that is particularly useful for Americans. Consider contrasts in expectations as to whether one should hold **technical** or **social** competence as a qualification for conducting business. Actually, most negotiators will need a mix of the two and will be flattered when either is recognized. But the mix tends to vary in emphasis from place to place, and counterparts from traditional societies may operate much more on the basis of their **social** competence: **who** they are, what their connections are, the social class they belong to, how formally educated they are, who they are related to. These are the qualifications by which they hold authority and get things done.

Most American negotiators, on the other hand, tend to occupy the far end of the range toward technical competence when credentials are checked for appointment to position and for assigning authority. Thus, they frequently find they are dealing with counterparts who place somewhat more stock on their social competence than seems reasonable to Americans. An underlying difference in this role definition helps explain some of the feeling of social distance in achieving rapport both within and without the negotiation process. It explains why subtle irritations result from mismatches in the way each side judges the credibility of the other. Much Mexican-American negotiation seems to be complicated by the intrusion of this cross-cultural reality.[7]

SECOND CONSIDERATION:
STYLES OF DECISION-MAKING

Obviously a negotiator's art must include an ability to anticipate the other side's decision-making process, and hopefully to influence it. In international negotiation this means taking into account contrasts in the "culture" of decision-making, that is, in the way officials and executives reach their institutional decisions and instruct their negotiators, as well as the more general cultural patterns by which individuals take on their personal styles of decision-making behavior. These contrasts probably pose the greatest problem when resident Americans work on an individual basis with their counterparts or with officials who preside over an area of specific concern, as for example, when dealing with the Director of Immigration, Minister of Public Works, a company comptroller, the Rector of a University, or even the manager of an automobile repair shop or a contractor.

Such individuals will normally reflect the mind-set of their institutional culture. Some of this might simply be preoccupations that arise from company or bureaucratic in-fighting or competition for budgets. But there is much that is less obvious—implicit assumptions and a sense of standard operating procedures, as well as more formal rules and regulations that become second-nature in the thinking of those whose careers are spent within the organizations and institutions in question. Thus contrasting institutional systems can introduce entirely different frames of reference for making decisions. Raymond Vernon, for instance, once noted that Americans and Russians carry contrasting implicit assumptions when "entrepreneurs" have to negotiate with **apparatchiks**. The problem is seen in making an export decision. To the American, "anything is permitted unless it has been restricted by the state." For the Soviet counterpart, "nothing is permitted unless it is initiated by the state."[8]

To an extent this is simply a study in comparative government and management, and the reader may prefer to categorize the problem in these terms. But however the cross-cultural perspective is defined, it is useful to pursue two essential questions:

(1) **How does the nature of a given nation's institutional culture produce a unique pattern of collective decision-making?**

(2) **In what way does a local culture affect an individual's decision-making style?**

Note that for the moment we are considering culture as a factor in determining **how** decisions are made, not the substance of them. Japan presents a classic case in this regard. There is a considerable literature on it, and we will give it greater attention here. But first, some notes from Mexico and France.

In Mexico, Americans find both a relatively centralized decision-making process and a decsion-making style which includes a greater projection of individual personality. It is a system in which decision goes from the top down. Its governing political party itself is centralized and secretive. Mexicans logically prefer to deal abroad at the higher levels of government and business and on a personal and private basis when problems must be addressed. It is normal for them to think of negotiating in terms of linking issues and making trade-offs—perhaps conceding a point on narcotics control in exchange for freer vegetable importation into the U.S. On the Mexican side there is someone in charge at the top who can orchestrate such positions. It is not surprising that they become frustrated in dealing with Americans whose system is based on bureaucratic compartmentalization of issues, with the bureaucrats in charge prepared to negotiate only in specified areas. American negotiators are preoccupied with coordination among their own divisions, agencies and interest groups that have some controlling influence over the issue at hand. For example, from a Rand Corporation discussion paper:

> "...the immigration issue alone regularly involves elements of Labor, HEW, Justice, INS, the Border Patrol, the Domestic Council, State, and Congress, not to mention labor unions, employer organizations, Chicano groups, the police and other private and state-level agencies."[9]

The balancing act required within the U.S. government to arrive at a position in relation to a single negotiation subject presents the American with problems enough. It is too much to try to make trade-offs **among** issues. Hence, to the Mexican it seems impossible to get a grip on a larger American decision-making process and get serious American attention to their overall problems and concerns. The end result is a built-in standoff in meshing negotiating gears. One side's view of negotiating objectives does not fit the other's. Even an American president cannot easily adjust an overall American position in the way that the Mexican president can.

In another mismatch of the systems, the American finds it hard to determine how much Mexican decision-making authority goes with which designated position. There, as in many of the more traditional systems, authority tends to reside somewhat more in the person than in the position, and an organization chart does little to tell the outsider just what leverage—**palanca**—the incumbent has. When the Mexican official or executive does hold authority, force of personality and personal connections tend to be key factors, although there are many notable exceptions. While the **caudillos**—the men on horseback—are gone, their style of decision-making lingers on in the culture, and an image of being a forceful personal decision-maker is part of the cultural basis for holding authority in the first place.

But this forceful decision-making is not cast in the same

mold as that of the successful executive who measures worthiness by goods produced and organizations efficiently managed. It is not decision-making derived from "the Protestant ethic and the spirit of capitalism." One observer has noted that in much of Southern Europe and Latin America the image of success is more related to having gained a reputation for and an ability to project an aura of personal public significance and power, of being one whose wisdom and leadership are sought after, one who is essential to a client group. **Holding** authority is the objective; delegating it would be giving away one's assets.[10]

Even a private secretary of a man with established authority within the Mexican system may be far more important in influencing a decision than an official in an equivalent position who lacks **palanca**. (People make careers in Mexico as private secretaries to key personalities; this is a highly significant role that is often overlooked.) The successful American, then, is the one who has had the time, experience or good advice, to gain a comprehensive knowledge of Mexican personalities, their ambitions, and the teams on which they play. One has to know this pattern well enough to know which official to go to—certainly which one not to overlook—in conducting business.

How does the American work with this system? Trying to influence the decision-making process is a delicate matter as Mexicans are especially sensitive to American attempts to manipulate their decisions. A sense of having been manipulated can produce negative, and from the point of view of an outsider, often irrational reactions. And they quickly spot a patronizing stance. However, a degree of cross-cultural adjustment has been achieved by a number of special negotiating mechanisms that have been worked out for handling on-going issues. Continuing Commissions have been particularly effective as, for example, the U.S.-Mexico Commission for Border Development and Friendship and the International Boundary and Water Commission. By being continuing bodies with members working with each other over time, an essential personal rapport can be generated, and a familiarity with the other side's decision-making process can be gained and appreciated. Established bi-national organizations provide still more opportunity for sustained personal rapport to develop.

On one-time issues with Mexico, behind-the-scenes exploration of mutual constraints and objectives, and reaching agreement with key personalities **before** they are faced with a U.S. position in a more formal setting, are more likely to be successful.

Turning to the French case, we find that, as might be expected, Americans report less difficulty in understanding **how** the French make their decisions than in understanding why the substance of their decisions cannot be more "reasonable." Some suggest the problem is a difference in the time-frame held in mind when decisions are made. The French start with a long-range view of their purposes and place lower priority on accommodation in short-range decisions to reach objectives which seem of little consequence. As Americans tend to focus on the short-term, it is harder for them to see that there might be, in fact, a design in French decisions.

Generally the French decision-making process presents few surprises if one makes a comparative study of American and French governmental, business and other national institutions. For example, note that the French executive branch of government has relatively more authority than in the U.S. or that a given substantive issue may be delegated to a differing combination of ministries and agencies. As in the United States, the coordination process in arriving at agreed positions is intricate and a matter of much internal negotiation. But it differs in specific detail, and this makes it easy for the American negotiator to miss the nuances of his counterpart's maneuvering in bureaucratic politics. As a result he may call too much public attention to an aspect of a French position that has been delicately arrived at, in the process threatening what may already have been the most favorable French position. Negotiating with the French seems to be an example of a case where the lack of large and obvious differences in decision-making style dulls sensitivity to the important ones that do exist.

American businesses report more difficulty in cooperative decision-making when they have to work outside Paris. Provincial French business organizations reflect more of their traditional and provincial business culture. Such matters as, for example, the way that executives relate to each other or the degree to which labor organizations affect policy present a challenge to the meshing of decision-making styles.

In turning to the decision-making structure in Japan, Americans sense that despite Japanese modernity, they really are dealing with something alien. The Japanese system disallows flexibility at the negotiating table and requires long periods of time to consider new proposals. It appears unapproachable to the outsider who hopes to influence the decision-making process or at least to inject pertinent information or to anticipate the direction in which decisions are moving.

In explaining the problem to an American audience, the president of a Japanese corporation suggested that perhaps the term "decision-making" is not applicable to the Japanese, that the concept as understood in the West involves so many difficult philosophical comparisons and contrasts in basic assumptions that it should not be used. Something like "direction-taking" might be better, for this would allow one to consider the consensus-building process in Japanese problem-solving and would avoid the notion of a decision being a finite and isolated act of executives that can set off a series of subsequent actions in an organization to support the will of management.[11] This counsel speaks directly to an American habitual desire to know **who** makes decisions, and it is precisely in this realm that Japanese institutional culture defies comparison. Even when explained, it all seems to go so much against common sense that the American finds it unbelievable and hard to take seriously.

The logic of Japanese decision-making contrasts not only with American, but with Mexican and French styles as well. For example, it is not one in which individual personalities stand out as in the Mexican. It is unique, for despite the hierarchial nature of Japanese society—consider the problems of learning all the honorifics needed to carry on polite conversation in the Japanese language—it is a decision-making process where ideas and supporting decisions tend to come from the bottom up, or at least from mid-level up, rather than from the top down. The negotiator speaks from the authority of a consensus—something that cannot be easily changed in the give-and-take of negotiation.

The thought patterns on which all this rests will be sketched out in the next section. But what are the elements in organizational practice that stand out?

First, the Japanese system is one in which the consensus-gathering process for adopting new policies or directions, and the preparation for carrying them out, go on, in effect, at the same time. Thus, while the process is exceedingly slow in producing conclusions, it is fast in implementation afterwards—somewhat the reverse of the American process where everyone down the line still has to be brought on board after the decision is made. Note the differences in the U.S. and elsewhere. Within the American bureaucracy it is often amazing how **little** ability a newly appointed director of an agency has to change ideas in his organization after deciding on a new program. This is true to a significant degree in business organizations as well. Bureaucrats have long practice in resisting such. In Mexico, they often cannot do much more than wait until the top man **does** decide. And in France, decision-making authority is distributed more throughout the civil service system. None of this matches the logic of the Japanese system.

In Japan, new initiatives depend heavily on middle-level technical experts, and their superiors tend to accept their judgements. Their accumulation of data and information serves both the deliberation process and implementation. This is where Americans doing the groundwork for negotiation feel themselves deluged with requests for information, often detailed beyond imaginable use, or at least beyond any use that Americans can see as needed at that stage. This, however, is the one stage at which the outsider can make an input; the rest of the decision-making process is closed except as a personal contact may be enjoyed at some point up the consensus cross-checking line.

Coordination of position among interested sub-sections of government or of corporations is slow, for appropriate equals must talk to equals. Subordinates must brief endlessly while their superiors use their networks of personal association to feel out the positions of the other players, or try to persuade without confrontation. This is the process hidden from the foreigner. After it is completed, top managers, even though perhaps the initiators of the whole process in the first place, end up serving as prestigeful representatives of the structure over which they preside, avoiding the stance of the dynamic decision-making executive.

Despite this apparent unobtrusiveness, the process is not necessarily secret or hidden from the Japanese public. On large national issues consensus deliberation is carried out in part in the public media as both intentional and unintentional trial balloons are raised, in effect adding channels for debate. The wider the range of interests concerned with an issue and the less the real consensus, the slower the decision-making process, and the greater the preference for ambiguous and imprecise decisions that facilitate harmony.

It should be noted that government and private industry also seek consensus on issues of mutual concern. Corporate leaders are frequently included in discussions of national policy from the beginning and contribute to the final decision—again, so that no one surprises anyone else.

So we see Japanese positions are laboriously determined. In negotiations they are not subject to sharp change—this requires going back through the process. As this approach stands in contrast to that of American negotiators who may not have fully made up their minds until they test out negotiating positions, it is not surprising that Americans consider the Japanese obstinate when they are able to take essentially only one position. In their eagerness to resolve problems, Americans are left either to acquiesce in the Japanese position or to retreat into a standoff. In any case, to the Japanese a negotiated agreement is seen as an indication of the direction to be taken, as noted above, with adjustments and modifications to be made according to conditions and consensus among the parties. Thus a U.S. expectation of contractual finality is uncongenial to Japanese institutional culture. And the Japanese inclination to suggest "sensible" changes after a contract is signed is seen from the U.S. side as devious.

When it comes to conducting more routine business when on assignment in Japan, the cultural problem with decision-making is resolved largely by working with an established cultural buffer zone. Perhaps more than in any other nation where cultures stand in sharp contrast, Japan has had to supply special people and techniques for working with American styles of decision-making and for bridging the gap with Japanese styles. The occupation period after World War II spawned a generation of officials and supporting staff whose mission in life was to work with outsiders—something that is still very unnatural for most Japanese managerial and executive level people. With this generation passing into retirement, their successors, while better able to work with foreign technology, may be less inclined to carry on with a deference to American approaches simply by force of habit. Still, Japan makes a conscious effort to supply the talent for dealing with foreigners, especially Americans.

The way for most outsiders to get things done in Japan, then, is through Japanese who are prepared to act as buffers. The Embassy and American official missions rely heavily on their local employees. American businesses do not attempt to become as deeply involved in Japan as they would elsewhere; they work through Japanese executives.

The problem, therefore,—and this will have application to some degree in many situations—is **to understand the go-between's problems when he plays this buffer role**. A minimum objective is to know enough about the differences in the way that decisions are made and processed so that the cultural broker in the middle is not presented with impossible tasks or that time constraints are not unrealistically set.

Generally, the best buffer is a person clearly identifiable with Japanese society. Only our best American language-trained personnel can do it well, and they have severe limitations. Interestingly, Americans of Japanese descent tend to be neither well accepted nor personally prepared to play this role. (And the same is true to a lesser extent for Mexican-Americans dealing officially in Mexico, according to some observers.)

THIRD CONSIDERATION:
HOW MUCH DOES "NATIONAL
CHARACTER" AFFECT NEGOTIATION?

For a variety of technical and research reasons, the term "national character" has not enjoyed the highest reputation among social scientists. But it might actually serve the negotiator's purposes better, for it can call attention both to the patterns of personality that negotiators tend to exhibit as products of their own society and to the collective concerns and outlooks that give a nation a distinctive "character" and outlook in international relationships.

We start by recalling the anthropological proposition that patterns of personality do exist for groups that share a common culture, that in the process of being socialized in a given society, the individual picks up the knowledge, the ideas, the beliefs and values, the phobias and anxieties of the group. Some of this is taught explicitly; most of it is absorbed subconsciously. Americans come to value time and efficiency, to place emphasis on the individual and individual achievement, and to love statistics. The Japanese as easily come to place emphasis on the group, to value and honor complex sets of obligations, to feel comfortable communicating in silence, and to recognize the virtues exemplified by the legendary forty-seven **ronin**. Mexicans learn to treat time less frenetically, to value human response and close personal relationships, and to more stoically accept fate than their northern neighbors. And the French present variations from American themes by differentiating more carefully between their public and private worlds, by seeing themselves as people of thought and reason, and by taking history more seriously. If one makes such comparisons on the basis of statistical averages or probability rather than as rigid formulas for understanding individual counterparts, the validity is more apparent.

In comparing national character, it must be recognized that fundamental belief systems can carry deep emotional charge and be highly resistant to change. The psychology of the many conflicts in the Middle East demonstrates this. Even outlooks on life and death are affected by culture. A few years ago a group of psychiatrists compared notes on their experience in Egypt and Israel during and after the October war. They found that there were widely differing patterns in public response to battlefield deaths. The Israelis were more shaken and more likely to take that factor into account in their policy debate.

How "rational" or "irrational" a society's beliefs are has little to do with their effectiveness as factors in perception and motivation of action. The counsel of the psychological anthropologist applies: while people may be alike in basic human qualities, they do not necessarily think alike. Even if sophisticated international negotiators could do so because of their immersion in an internationalized culture, their clients would still reflect the special emotional and cognitive patterns of their respective societies. It is this reality that makes international negotiation such a special art.

For the purposes of negotiation, it is useful to recognize the areas in which the possibility of national character contrasts needs to be explored. These include matters of national images, values and assumptions which affect the substance of negotiation, and styles of reasoning. Therefore, discussion will be organized around several lead questions:

1. How do national self-images and images of the other party affect negotiation?

No other set of psychological factors was mentioned as frequently by persons who contributed to this study as the perceptions their counterparts held of their country's international position or of their special qualities as a nation.

The context usually was negotiation with the United States, of course, so therefore perceptions of the U.S. and of U.S. intentions were next most often noted. Interviewees who became still more analytical included American self-perceptions and American images of the other, recognizing that such images are often carried more out of awareness than American negotiators recognize.

French self-images seemed to stand out especially as a factor in negotiation. Their preoccupation with French culture and the French language would be familiar to the reader. Projection of French culture is almost a priority consideration in French foreign policy. They see nothing wrong with French cultural imperialism. One observer noted that a French state visit to Romania was seen as successful when an agreement was signed to do no more than increase the teaching of French in local schools. The French hold an acute consciousness of history—from the French point of view—and with this the glory of France as a unique force in Western civilization. This component of their national character was a prime factor in de Gaulle's appeal to the French public and in his ability to provide a sense of self-assurance in difficult times. De Gaulle noted that France has been outstanding even in its defeats.

It follows that the French tend to perceive themselves as holding a special position in the international arena. France is not simply another European country—it is France. The country has a mystique that is part of the French soul. Its policy-makers do not need to apologize for taking actions that they see to be strictly in France's self interest. They do not hesitate in being the exception. One person noted that he could not imagine a French leader's self-image allowing him to say, as President Kennedy did at the Berlin Wall, "Ich bin ein Berliner."

In its uniqueness France has seen itself playing such special international roles as being a bridge between China and the West or having a special mentor relationship with the developing world. The French sense of close alliance with the United States runs deep and they usually do expect to extend close cooperation, but they do not hold United States leadership in awe. Stanley Hoffman notes that they expect the U.S., like France, to act in its self-interest, and are not impressed by American declarations of altruistic motives.[12] The French appreciated Marshall Plan assistance, but do not now see that this has left an obligation on their part. Where their self-image may suffer from less than complete assurance is in the realm of technological accomplishment. As this stands out as a standard of prestige in contemporary world affairs, the French apparently feel some anxiety that they might be vulnerable—although they would rather by judged by other standards of civilization.

For Mexico, matters of national identity could hardly differ more. History is their problem rather than a source of assurance. Throughout their independence the United States has been the overpowering reality and the mirror by which Mexico was always seen to have a lower national stature. While a blend of distinguished Indian tradition, and a far-reaching social revolution have provided a satisfying distinctness to the Mexican sense of self, the consciousness of being "so far from God and so close to the United States" has molded many self-perceptions. Perhaps most important, awareness of the reciprocal image that Americans hold of Mexico and Mexicans, combined with a sense of having been cavalierly used, has heightened the defensive sensitivity to further dignity-shattering actions on the part of the colossus to the north.

One observer noted that the maximum time that even a friendly Mexican could spend with an American without bringing up some aspect of what the United States has done to Mexico is about two hours. However this might be, in virtually every negotiation, interaction has been complicated by sensitivity to their perceived dependent relationship with the United States and their long memory of patronizing and demeaning actions taken by the U.S. as a government, by American companies, and by Americans as individuals. Even after Americans think that they have taken this into account, they find they have not appreciated the depth and emotional charge of the outlook. Nor do they appreciate how subtly their own perceptions have become ingrained. The result is that they unwittingly display still more behavior that can be taken as patronizing or as discounting the Mexican's worth. Even President Carter's apparently honest attempt to be informally friendly and talk as an equal backfired when he joked about "Montezuma's revenge" in remarks made during his 1979 visit to Mexico. A construction company's boast regarding the efficiency of a new fence being constructed along the border or tactics used in policing illegal immigrants can set off instant public indignation in Mexico.

How closely a Mexican identifies with the United States can be a delicate matter, although less so in cities like Monterrey and the business sections of border communities. A Binational Center Director noted that in dealing with his Board of Directors he had to be sure that he did not force his cooperating Mexican members too far and too often out on a limb with their fellow-citizens by expecting them to defend the Center against criticism or by making it appear that they were serving the American Director instead of the other way around.

It is also reported, however, that some Mexicans have learned that this imbalance is not necessarily to their disadvantage. Americans, they find, are sensitive to being called insensitive. Therefore it is useful especially in business agreements to play the position of the weaker partner in negotiation, of the side that needs special consideration for being disadvantaged, even to be able to flatter the stronger partner's capacity to provide extra help. Where this approach crosses the line from being a sincerely felt position to calculated tactics is not easily determined. Presumably as petroleum resources strengthen Mexico's position, Americans will be less inclined to yield to such tactics.

But the basic Mexican outlook is that they do not want to be beholden to the U.S. more than is absolutely necessary. The fact that AID and the Peace Corps have never been accepted there, as they have in other parts of Latin America, or that any private philanthropy that appears as patronizing is rejected, demonstrates the wariness. This outlook is more than a problem of poor versus rich; it is a matter of interpreting why the rich are rich and the poor are poor. From the way that history is taught in the Mexican classroom to the memory of expropriating the petroleum companies (1938), through a revolution in which privilege was denounced, to the political persuasions of university students—the U.S. has been held up as the source of Mexican misfortune. It takes a lot of reasonableness to over-ride this pervasive pattern of perceptions.

Another source of sensitivity comes from having to live in the shadow of American technological achievement and with the Americans' quickness to judge the Mexican in that comparison. Stereotypes result of which the Mexican can hardly be unaware. President Lopez Portillo has made specific reference to these stereotypes as an impediment to understanding. Since such a large part of American-Mexican negotiation involves technological matters and standards of performance, these images have far-reaching effects.

The Japanese present quite another pattern of self-images and self-perceptions as related to the U.S. Actually, to many ordinary Japanese, the very idea of having a "self-image" may be rather abstract, for unlike Americans, they constitute a highly homogeneous society and have little reason, normally, to take outside comparative references into account. For much of Japanese history, foreigners were considered to be so far outside the various recognized categories of social relationships that for all practical purposes they were outside the human universe. Yet at the same time, concern for world opinion did have an appeal and was a strong motivating force for collective performance in rebuilding after World War II and the humiliation of defeat.

Unlike the Mexicans, Japanese have little trouble in coping with the fact that America is a superior power. Perhaps distance helps, but a key factor is said to be a Japanese readiness to extend to the international arena their view of hierarchy and place. There is more inclination to see established hierarchy as affording the security of known position and promoting harmony. The war settled what the order was. So any problem the Japanese have with U.S. power in an unbalanced relationship turns on the way that power is managed in the relationship, and not, as has been suggested, on the slowness of the U.S. in recognizing Japan's rising status as an **economic** power.

Therefore, when Japan perceives the American position negatively, it is a matter of sensitivity to being ill used, taken for granted, or having their interests ignored by the power on which they depend. Thus their "shock" in not being informed in advance of the opening contact with China was only partly a shock over substance. It was more a reaction to what was perceived to be inappropriate unilateral behavior on the part of a superior power with whom they thought they had a special understanding.

In contrast to the Mexican situation, Japanese do not necessarily find a dependency relationship undignified or undesirable. Japanese culture provides for this in the **amae** concept in personal relationships, as when a student is dependent on a teacher, a child on its parents, or an employee on his employer. American benevolence in exercising superior power after the war made the **amae** relationship rather natural.[13] The trouble is that as other relationships demand American attention or as Americans see little need to be Japan's patron today, the Japanese request, so often reported by negotiators, that the United States be understanding of special Japanese circumstances, is increasingly resisted. The Japanese reaction to this rejection is cast in a very different psychological mold than that found in American-Mexican negotiation relationships.

Japan's self image also includes a recognition of racial and cultural uniqueness. Japanese moving for the first time into international cirlces tend to be inexperienced in carrying this identity outside their homogeneous society, and it is the cause of some anxiety. The possibility of discrimination is a twofold problem: the unpleasantness of discrimination itself when it is, in fact, encountered and the uncertainty as to when it actually is present and the form it might take. When among Westerners, the racial and cultural distinctness is too obvious to easily ignore. Further, in their international dealings the pressure is usually on **them** to make the social adaptations, not the other way around, and this poses an added burden on both their capabilities for negotiation and on their self-image. All this gives their internationally-experienced officers and executives who are comfortable in managing their racial difference a special responsibility and status, a fact not always appreciated in negotiation situations.[14]

Before leaving the discussion of national images as a function of culture and national character, it is well to point out that observers stress the need for Americans to be aware of the psychological baggage they too carry, both their own self-images and those they hold of negotiating opposites. In the cases explored here, it has been obvious that American images of the French, Mexicans and Japanese have affected the dynamics of negotiation on both formal and informal levels. When these images were out-of-step either with reality or the other's image, they not only gave needless offense, but, more important, they clouded judgment of the counterpart's position and intentions. They have led to misattribution of motives and sometimes to misperception of tactics and strategy.

For illustrative purposes, here are just a few items that seem to relate to an American negotiating style. They are presented more to establish this kind of introspection as logical procedure than to delve very far into American self-images.

—American negotiators frequently and necessarily see themselves as basically **multi-lateral** negotiators, that is they see American interests and implications of the subject at hand as spread out over a range of countries, of which the counterpart of the moment's country is only one. Thus there is a mathematical standoff in outlook: the counterpart is interested specifically in one-to-one negotiation with the

United States; the American sees the other nation as one of many with similar matters pending with the U.S. The American's "big picture" is a perspective that most probably will clash with that held by his opposite. In business negotiations this grand outlook may be less prevalent, though in the case of major industries and American-based multinationals, it no doubt still applies.

—Americans carry a leadership role in their heads and tend to see American objectives as coinciding with those of a larger world community including the counterpart's country. While this assumption may or may not be accurate, the outlook affects American style. The French and Mexicans, for example, tend to be unimpressed, while the Japanese are more appreciative.

—Americans see themselves as models of modernity and technological success and, therefore, as advisors. This seems to give a license to prescribe, an approach that is taken whether invited or not in many negotiations.

—Among other kinds of "imperialism," Americans have been accused of "moral imperialism." This may be the identification of a particularly hard-to-take attitude of self-righteousness Americans are perceived sometimes as carrying into negotiations.

—Americans also see themselves playing an international role as problem-solvers working in everyone's best interests. They therefore expect a degree of deference to this role in negotiation and assume that everyone's final position will be arrived at during negotiation. But an American's sense of problem-solving may be interpreted as an attempt to manipulate.

2. What specific values and implicit assumptions do negotiators carry with them?

Rarely in communication do two people talk about precisely the same subject, for effective meaning is flavored by the inter-related elements that make up each person's own cognitive world. In international negotiation this translates into a question of anticipating which culturally-related ideas, values, or implicit assumptions tend to explain how the subject at hand is most likely to be understood by a person socialized in a given culture. Such cultural conditioning might not hold each individual in a cognitive straight jacket, but the probability that it will have a basic effect deserves exploration.

Certainly the resources are not available for a full analysis in the cases of Japan, Mexico and France, but a half dozen samples of conflicting values and assumptions might be useful.

In many instances, implicit assumptions regarding **ethics** and **ethical behavior** lie near or just underneath the surface of discussion. Because these idea patterns carry emotional charge, they are harder to deal with, and, beyond their impact on the substance of discussion, they affect the level of confidence and trust. One sample is what specialists on Japan have cited as an American problem with Japanese "situation ethics." That is, as Japanese appear to take different positions in different settings, the American sees duplicity and lack of individual integrity rather than normal behavior in a consensus society. Japanese, on the other hand, have a problem trying to anticipate the effect of Christian-based ethics and the importance of principles in American positions. They see Americans unnecessarily rejecting sound practical ideas simply because they violate principles that are not usual to Japanese ways of thinking.

Americans frequently find their moral fine tuning challenged in deciding what foreign behavior constitutes bribery or corruption. In most societies, including the United States, the lines that divide customary perquisites and expected forms of recompense for services from unacceptable abuse are often defined more by culturally-patterned tacit understanding than by the same culture's formal or public codes. This does not eliminate a sense of right and wrong or the subjective feelings that go with ethical issues; it just makes it harder to understand it all cross-culturally. From negotiating gift bottles of Christmas cheer at the customs house to agreeing to special expediters' commissions, finding the formula is rarely an emotionally neutral process. The problem can be seen in mirror image as foreign business or government representatives try to work the gray area in the U.S.

Differing values placed on agreements and contracts and differing assumptions as to the way they should be honored are prime examples of the psycho-cultural problem. Americans take them seriously indeed and assume that American credibility in world affairs depends on the strictest adherence. Russian backsliding in this regard is seen as further evidence of the immorality of their system. But Japanese also take a differing view. In fact, traditionally, Japanese have preferred to operate on the basis of understanding and social trust with the need for a more formal contract considered a rather unfortunate circumstance. They even point out that they have an economic advantage in that their system is more efficient with less time and expense wasted on the lawyers and law suits that go with a contract-obsessed society such as the U.S.

In any event they tend to see a contract or formal agreement as the beginning of an adaptive process rather than the end of one. They assume that changes and adjustments will naturally be made in good faith as developments or circumstances indicate. This makes the American assume that the agreement was made in bad faith to begin with. In conducting modern business the Japanese are adjusting to the world of contractual obligation, of course, but the psychology lingers on.

In Mexico the outlook swings a few degrees in another direction. With some admitted exaggeration we might say that formal agreements there are works of art and expressions of the ideal, and should be appreciated as such. They, like laws, do not necessarily apply all the time and should not be expected to cover the detailed practical world, which is not a work of art, or situations in which certain human considerations take precedence. Again, Mexicans are very competent in international business and diplomacy, but there is less joy for the Mexican in the cold contract than for the American who finds his security in the exact and impersonal wording.

Any contrasts in the value placed on **compromise** itself certainly would bring cultural relativity to bear on the negotiation process. Americans are among the most enthusiastic proponents of compromise. It was compromise that made America great! It is the natural way to do business; it has a moral aura that helps one live with what might otherwise be a morally ambiguous concession. But the Japanese are not normally prepared to compromise without going back to the drawing board, and the Mexicans and French see less virtue in compromising **per se**. To the French, a well-reasoned position does not call for compromise unless the reasoning is faulty. And that can be discussed. Even when a compromise is pragmatically although reluctantly reached, the French negotiator still gains some satisfaction in recalling the correctness of the preferred uncompromised position. To the Mexican, compromise translates more into a matter of honor—which is held in very high regard. When the American feels that progress has been made with a compromise, the Mexican may feel that something has been lost in his context of values which stresses a kind of dignity and integrity that is upheld precisely in **not** being compromised. Dueling, it may be recalled, was much more the norm in Latin America than in the United States.

American informality in down-playing status, in using first names, in dress, casualness, impatience with formalities, and so forth, places Americans toward one end of a range of international negotiating behavior. Their egalitarian assumptions have long been a threat to international protocol; typically the American has to rise to the protocol occasion, and relatively few of our negotiators carry it off well. This sometimes contributes to confused signals or disturbing "noise" in the communication background (as discussed further in the next section).

Other areas of underlying assumptions relate to the negotiation style as well. For example, should negotiating positions be based on legal precedence, on expert opinion and technical data, on amity, on reciprocal advantage? Is it normal procedure to try to package and sell an argument with visual aids and advertising techniques? How much is deviousness sanctioned in a "buyer beware" approach? Is bargaining a pleasure or a chore? How much value is placed on time and efficiency in the negotiation process versus social amenities and ceremony? Does one prefer privacy and secrecy or openness? Is frankness and directness a virtue? (It is not to Mexicans in formal encounters, apparently, nor to Japanese at any time.) When is humor appropriate, or for that matter, what constitutes humor, especially when directed toward individuals?

More profound areas might reflect differing ideological assumptions and values or different conceptions of social purpose. Is competition "good"? Does the well-being of the individual or that of the group take precedence when property rights, profit, law or government policy come into discussion? What loyalties are to be honored first in determining how official position is to be used? How is national interest defined and when does it take priority? When are revolutionary goals simply rhetoric and when are they controlling and deeply felt commitments? When is an issue a religious one? When does unthinkably immoral behavior in one society become thinkable in another? Terrorism or the holding of hostages forces one to be analytically responsive to questions of this emotional depth.

3. Are there cultural differences in styles of logic and reasoning and therefore in styles of persuasion?

International negotiators frequently find that discussions are impeded because the two sides seem to be pursuing different paths of logic. This breakdown may result from the way that issues are conceptualized, the way evidence and new information are used, or the way one point seems to lead to the next. Here we come to one of the most intriguing but least researched aspects of the cultural dimension in negotiation. Do cultures, and perhaps their languages also, tend to impart to the members of the society distinctive ways of putting ideas together, associating causes and effects, seeking knowledge and understanding, using evidence and reasoning? Could it be that a line of reasoning that would be persuasive in the U.S. would be ineffective in another culture? In any event, does this impede modern international communication? Generally, thoughtful observers say yes, but in scientific terms the subject is only minimally understood. Because of the potential importance of these questions for understanding the international negotiation process, they are worth posing as a matter of needed inquiry and as a subject for curiosity on the part of the sensitive negotiator.[15] From our sample countries, a few tentative observations can be made.

In this study the matter came up principally in relation to French use of what is popularly referred to as Cartesian logic. Rather imprecisely defined, the idea is that one reasons from a starting point based on what is known, and then pays careful attention to the logical way in which one point leads to the next, and finally reaches a conclusion regarding the issue at hand. The French also assign greater priority than Americans do to establishing the principles on which the reasoning process should be based. Once this reasoning process is under way, it becomes relatively difficult to introduce new evidence or facts, most especially during a negotiation. Hence the appearance of French inflexibility, and the need to introduce new information and considerations early in the game. All this reflects the tradition of French education and becomes the status mark of the educated person. In an earlier era observers made such sweeping generalizations as: "The French always place a school of thought, a formula, convention, **a priori** arguments, abstraction, and artificiality above reality; they prefer clarity to truth, words to things, rhetoric to science..."[16] Despite modern management and technical application in the French bureaucracy, some feel that vestiges of this style of deliberation are still encountered.

Consider the case of American versus Mexican logic. The American is persuaded by expert opinion and supporting hard evidence and uses such in presenting a position in negotiation. Mexicans, however, are less likely to be equally impressed. They generally prefer a **deductive** approach as opposed to the American inclination toward the **inductive**. Like other Latin Americans and other nationalities as well— some authorities would include the French and the Russians—the emphasis is placed on starting with the most general aspects by defining issues, categorizing them, and deciding on the main principle. Once this is done, then logic follows along to the conclusion with less attention to supporting evidence. Or new evidence may be interpreted in the light of the main principle already determined.[17]

This contrast in approach is sometimes found in UN debate. Americans become irritated with the time taken in argument over which principle applies, to which UN committee an issue falls, or the exact wording of a title to be assigned to a new issue. The Americans want to concentrate on the facts available, to look for cause and effect, and to get on to problem-solving.

Tentatively, Mexican reasoning may also be more complex because it incorporates some of the Spanish tradition of placing more emphasis on contemplation and intuition. In this regard Mexican thought is somewhat similar to Japanese in that emotion, drama and feeling play a larger part as contrasted to American considerations of efficiency, scientific method and practical application or the colder logic and reasoning of the French. One observer noted that Japanese negotiators tend not to be convinced by hypothetical reasoning, or, as noted above, justification by principles. They do appreciate objective description and data from which conclusions are directly obvious.[18]

These questions in the study of culture pose an inquiry at the most abstract level and are least subject to observation. It is not likely that most negotiators will have occasion to follow their counterpart's thought process through from its base in philosophy, religion, and implicit methodology. But the line of questioning can be placed on our agenda. Much is to be learned by looking for the patterns of reasoning reflected in literature and aesthetics and in the way that discussion is structured and phrased in everyday social situations. The area specialist with time and a bent for philosophy may find this cross-cultural dimension revealing and of practical application in crossing negotiation bridges.

In a study of this scope, it can only be reported that there is a reality here to be taken into account. The negotiator reflects it when he is happily surprised that his counterpart "thinks just like an American." Japanese apparently have this objective in mind when they send their future foreign service officers to such American colleges as Williams or Swarthmore for several years of study. Other countries demonstrate that they have learned something about this when they choose negotiators who can indeed think like Americans when dealing with the U.S.

There was the time, for example, when Panama sent a negotiating team to Washington to try to gain American approval for extending their national air route beyond Miami to New York. The team consisted of one man, a graduate of a ranking American business school. He quickly explained that from an economic point of view and by the usual considerations for justifying air traffic routes, he had no case and would not pretend to have one. He said that Panama did, nevertheless, understand the economic importance of Panama to American carriers and did have compelling nationalistic reasons for wanting to see its flag on the big route. He would be at his hotel and would appreciate being informed when it was worked out. This Panamanian was extraordinarily successful as compared with another team in town at the same time with the same purpose, but with a more typically Latin American approach and line of reasoning much less adapted to the American mentality.

FOURTH CONSIDERATION: COPING WITH CROSS-CULTURAL "NOISE"

It is not a very precise term, but "noise" has been used by communication analysts to call attention to the fact that background distractions which have nothing to do with the substance of a "message" nevertheless have to be taken into account if one wishes to understand complications in the communication process. Sometimes this distraction really is noise, or it might be the presence of other people, a poor telephone connection, or habits and idiosyncrasies of the communicators that bother one party or the other.

The noise concept is particularly useful in cross-cultural communication, for a whole new range of "noisy" elements reflecting cultural difference may be introduced to add to the strain of transmitting intended meaning. Such factors affect negotiation, especially in less cosmopolitan and less formal situations and certainly in the daily routine of doing business in another country. They deserve attention.

Cross-cultural "noise" can derive from gestures, or behavior which seems overly—or insufficiently—courteous, or clothing, or office surroundings that do not feel right for the occasion. The confusion comes, of course, because such surprises conflict with expectations and lead to misinterpretation of the situation or the intent of one's respondent or the meaning of the message itself.

Or they simply make it more difficult to pay attention to the main subject. One of the classics in this category is the distraction posed when the normal speaking distance between two people is violated in a cross-cultural encounter. The reader almost certainly has been reminded of this; it was first observed by anthropologist Edward Hall when he was on the staff of the Foreign Service Institute in the early 1950's. It was presented in his book **The Silent Language** and has been taught by FSI linguists since that time.[19]

Mexicans stand closer, Japanese further away. The emotional alarm that is set off when one's distance barrier is broken is an excellent reminder of the unnerving potential of such behavioral mismatches and also of the degree to which an individual can be entirely unaware of culturally-acquired practices until they surface in a cross-cultural situation. When emotions are involved, such as anxiety regarding intentions, disgust, modesty, etc., the challenge to maintain an even intellectual keel is still greater.

It is important to recall that the American's own behavior, especially informal behavior, has as much potential for making noise as that which the American faces. Some of the behaviors most often mentioned as distracting in cross-cultural situations are slouching, chewing gum, using a first name too soon, displaying the soles of one's shoes in a respondent's face, forgetting titles, starting speeches with jokes, inappropriate clothing, overly friendly approaches to the opposite sex, speaking too loudly, being too egalitarian with the wrong people, working with one's hands and carrying bundles, and tipping too much. There are many more.

Usually such things are not mentioned. Often they are simply part of "foreign" behavior and discounted accordingly. But there was, for example, the case of a Binational Center Director who was admonished by a member of his Chilean Board of Directors for ungentlemanly behavior when, in a tight budget situation, he proceeded to lead his local employees in painting the Center themselves. Status, role, and behavior seemed mixed up. Often reaction to behavior which "loses something in translation" is amusement, as in the case of the hand gesture which turns out to be obscene in local symbolism. But it is noise nonetheless, and it may be that humor at an unplanned moment, and particularly indecent humor, may derail the message that is intended.

The reader is, or will be, acquainted with this facet of the cross-cultural communication task by being a good observer and reasonably sensitive. Most competent language courses provide specific introductions to the subject as related to the people whose language is being studied. The significance of all this in negotiation is that the way that parties respond to each other is already in delicate balance. Consequently, introducing a little bit of psychological distortion in the form of ill-defined irritants or subtle bases for misperception can go a long way in producing unanticipated or negative consequences. Negotiators with limited international experience are most likely to be thrown off course by cross-cultural noise, both Americans and their counterparts.

A few samples from the case study countries might add illustration, even if rather randomly selected.

Perhaps the most unnerving form of Japanese "noise" is silence! Long pauses are normal in Japanese conversation both before responding and in the middle of a developing thought. To an American in such a situation, fifteen seconds can be a very long time, and panic tends to set in to fill the conversation vacuum. Further, Japanese forms of polite behavior tend to confuse Americans even though they rarely find themselves having to match bow for bow. Japanese politeness seems artificial to the Americans, as is also the case of the more formal European and Latin American behavior. Japanese attempts to avoid giving offense leave Americans with little feedback—they do not know how their messages are being received. Most difficult of all is knowing when the answer is "no." In fact, an internationally-wise Japanese has written a book for American businessmen to help them understand Japanese ways. The title is **Never Take Yes for an Answer.**[20] Japanese use of smiles and even laughter to signal shyness or embarrassment visibly confuses Americans.

In turn, American directness, display of emotion, and overbearing manner in trying to sell a point may signal a lack of self-control and therefore untrustworthiness. At the least it signals lack of "sincerity"—a Japanese mark of confidence.

The Mexican also avoids saying "no." The problem is to read the expressions and the qualifications which mean "no," even though the words say or imply "yes." Mexicans use some physical contact to signal confidence, such as a hand on the upper arm. Americans who are standoffish from the **abrazo** are probably a bit hard to take; they have signaled a certain coolness. Americans may have difficulty playing the high social status role that goes with important position in societies such as Mexico. There is an art to being waited on and deferred to while at the same time being protective of the personal dignity of people in lower social position. American expressions of impatience and irritation in Mexico when things do not work or delays are encountered create considerable "noise"—both figuratively and actually. Mexican practices relating to the role of women create their share of noise too.

As might be expected, noise problems do not stand out very clearly in French-American communication. Differences are not great, and the sense of "foreign" behavior is subdued. However, subtleties can create difficulties precisely because they are only variations on a theme and therefore not easily identified. The slight difference as to when one should start using a first name or the informal versus the formal form of "you" is a nuance that is not easily grasped and taken into account as a cross-cultural reality. The meaning of who picks up the check, just how one is addressed, the degree to which friends and family enter into business relationships, what can be criticized by an outsider, what response is in fact impolite—such matters have a cross-cultural dimension even between generally similar societies.

Can one be too cautious in trying to cope with this aspect of cross-cultural communication? In the world of international negotiation, it probably can be overdone if in the process one becomes too preoccupied with the endless small possibilities for misinterpreted behavior and as a result pays too little attention to the more basic cultural factors that affect the substance of negotiation. Still, ignoring the "noise" that might complicate an already delicate balance of negotiating factors is at the least short-sighted, and tuning in on what might appear to be superficial cultural manifestations can often lead to more profound insights into the counterpart's psychological environment.

FIFTH CONSIDERATION:
TRUSTING INTERPRETERS
AND TRANSLATORS

Usually the first—and sometimes the only—thought given to making the transition from domestic to international negotiation is to arrange for translation services. And as English is rapidly become an international language in business, technological and scientific circles, even the need to concern oneself with language difference appears to be reduced. The evidence is, however, that negotiators typically treat the translation and interpretation problem much too naively and prosaically. When translation is used, the process is seen as essentially mechanical. You put an idea in here and it comes out there. Some negotiators even see a tactical advantage in working through interpreters because it gives them more time to think about the next statement.

It was interesting to note that among officers interviewed in the course of this study, those with no foreign language ability tended to believe that language translation presented little problem. Those who did speak French, Spanish or Japanese saw distinct impediments in understanding despite the skill of interpreters. In any event the sense of unquestioned assurance with which otherwise cautious officers use interpreters is remarkable.

The fundamental problem is that language and culture are so intimately tied together that the negotiator has to ask: **What are the actual limits in translating ideas, concepts, meaning and nuance?** In international negotiation it is often the **latent** meaning—the way things are understood the next day, or the next year—that determines the effectiveness of an agreement reached. The more abstract the subject and the greater the contrasts in culture and national experience, the more probable it will be that over-confidence in the interpretation and translation process will pose a potential pitfall.

In the case of negotiating across English-French interpretation, cultural differences are fewer and abstract ideas are more or less similar. Further, French has been a prime international language for centuries, and interpretation to and from English has become a well-established practice. Yet experts tell us that more often than recognized, even the best translations are not exactly equivalent. For example on a somewhat philosophical level, Salvador de Madariaga, a senior internationalist and Spanish diplomat, wrote in his famous **Frenchmen, Englishmen, Spaniards** that an expression like **avoir raison** is not quite the same idea as to **be** right—"to have" versus "to be." He also suggests that English is the language of the man of action; French of the man of thought and that therefore the two languages have to reflect differing interpretations of daily life as well as international issues.[21]

Madariaga's analysis is debated, but in virtually all other pairings of languages, the equivalence-in-translation difficulty increases, sometimes to very significant proportions as in the case of Japanese.

Apparently interpretation problems were monumental in Viet Nam. It might be recalled that it was a Foreign Service Institute linguist who, while watching the evening news, discovered that a Vietnamese interpreter had simply given up when trying to bridge the gap between a CBS reporter and a Vietnamese villager. The TV audience watched the reporter ask a question, heard it go back and forth between the interpreter and the villager, and then heard the answer back in English. What the interpreter had done was simply ask the villager to count to ten, which he did. Then the interpreter reported what the villager **might** have said had he been able to understand the abstract ideas in the original question.

One's sympathy must be with the interpreter who faced an impossible task. The life experiences of the reporter and the villager, and their languages as reflections of culture, presented too great a contrast. While this is an extreme case, it is worth observing how frequently an interpreter is casually presented with jargon and culture-bound phrases that defy finding equivalent meanings: "get on the ball," "go for broke," "come to the bottom line."

The task for the negotiator, then, if effective communication is to sustain the negotiation process, is to make the best possible use of translation and interpretation resources. A look at some of the main problem areas might be helpful. A few lead questions follow:

1. **What is the subjective meaning on each side of a translated item?** For example, in Spanish the subjective meaning of **discutir** is not exactly the same as "discuss"—it has a more confrontational connotation. The Japanese equivalent of "individualistic" has a negative nuance while in English it is positive.

This is illustrated nicely by following a rather simple procedure an applied psychologist has used to explore effective meaning. It might be kept in mind the next time one is faced with an interpretation situation. He simply presents a selected sample of speakers of each language with a word or phrase—"educated," "government," "capitalistic system," "public interest." Then the subjects are asked to free associate with that cue word or phrase in their respective languages. They write down whatever comes to mind in one minute. When this data is organized the results are striking. We find that while in English "educated" means schools and classes, academic achievement, etc., in Spanish it includes the idea of a well-bred, sensitive, polite and decent person. The point is that whether one is writing it all down for the psychologist or not, this free association process is going on as each listener assigns meaning to what has been heard on his or her end of a translation.[22]

When meaning is further modified by gestures, tone of voice, cadence, asides and double-meanings which do not enter into translation, the problem is compounded.

Even when interpretation and translation do not appear to

be needed, there can be difficulties in the effective communication of meaning. When someone is speaking English as a **second** language, the tendency is to retain the subjective meaning of the native language—at least until experience is so accumulated that that person also **thinks** in the second language. English speakers do the same thing, of course, when speaking other languages. Hence, there is a good chance that people will not be speaking with the same meaning even when they are speaking the same language, and most especially when that language was learned in an artificial environment such as a classroom. The implication of this is that negotiators not only have to question whether their meaning will be transmitted through interpretation and translation, but also whether it will be communicated when the respondent is speaking the negotiator's own language as a second language.

2. **What will happen in interpretation if an idea or concept does not exist in the other culture?** How often this happens is the subject of much debate, and unfortunately the problem is relatively little investigated despite its importance. It is easier to simply acknowledge that a statement does not translate exactly and go on, or an interpreter might try to add explanation. When accurate communication is an essential in negotiation, this is risky. When a thought loses something in translation, that is probably the point to dig in and find out what it was that was lost, for it is precisely in those instances in which cultures do not have equivalent conceptions that the two sides in a discussion find themselves talking past each other. For example, there was no word for "democracy" when Japan was exposed to the West. Something had to be created out of three written characters to produce something like "peopleness" or populism. Usage may now make the gap smaller, but the communication problem presented is clear.

Those who study national character have been fond of the example presented in the very English (and American) notion of "fair play." It seems to have no exact equivalent in any other language. In French, word and concept were adopted together as **le fer plé**. In Spanish, **juego limpio** has been tried for application in sports, but it fails to transmit most of the basic thought. Generally, this is a culture-bound idea. How, then, can the American negotiator expect "fair play" from his opposite?

Like other people, we also sometimes borrow words with concept: "tortilla" and "sukiyaki" are in our English dictionary. Much diplomatic terminology comes directly from French. Sometimes having no equivalent can be an advantage, to be sure, as in new technological terminology or concepts in economics and business. Then there is reason to explain fully, and understanding can proceed with the problem of meaning having been met directly and solved.

Actually, Americans may find that the difficulty posed by inexact equivalents will be greatest when an idea is expressed by the **other** side for which there is no match in English. In that case the interpreter does the best possible, the Americans supply their own **assumed** meaning, and then, unless the meaning is very unclear, never know how much communication damage has been suffered. Even everyday Spanish words like **simpatico** or a Japanese word like **sumimasen**—something in the range of "excuse me"—fail safe passage. And a Japanese idea like **girl** (a special kind of obligation) or **haragei** (consensus-oriented talking around a point in bargaining) requires more study than the brief explanation of an interpreter to establish real meaning. Where translation goes from English to the other language, the American may more easily sense that there might be an uncertain equivalent.

3. **Do languages have built-in styles of reasoning that resist translation?** That is, do they sometimes differ enough in structure and in their format for sequence and interconnection of ideas that their speakers will be led to unique patterns of thinking and conceptualization? Earlier, we suggested that patterns of logic do differ by culture, whatever the part that language plays. This question is rather too abstruse for most negotiators' tastes. But if this kind of contrast does

exist, it would significantly affect how well abstract ideas can be communicated through an interpreter. For the American this might apply most to cases where non-Indo-European languages are involved. Specialists do not hold uniform opinions on this matter, but Edmund Glenn, a social scientist dedicated to this kind of inquiry, who also served for many years as Chief of the Department of State Language Services Division, insists that it is a valid concern and that interpreters often do have difficulty in transmitting the logical thrust of key statements. This is especially true when abstract subjects are being discussed, as is typically the case in international negotiation—analyses of situations, plans, institutions, economic forces, or international strategy. For example, the cause and effect emphasis implicit in English structure with its accompanying facility for expressing complexities of past, present and future action, might not easily match the framework of another language such as Arabic.[23]

Japanese scholars have suggested that Japanese and English differ in important ways as related to conducting dialogue or discussion. Japanese leads its user to decide **what** something is rather than **why** it should be that way. It presents a conclusion, not grounds for a back-and-forth debate or abstract questioning. There seem to be leaps in logic, rather than a process that goes with a Western use of dialogue. There is a distrust of attempts to use language to build a case for a given view of an issue. If this is true, the implications for presenting and discussing positions in negotiation would be substantial.[24]

In cases such as the above, the end result may be that while the interpreter can convey what is being expressed on a detail-by-detail basis, the intended thrust is lost as the two sides find that they are not operating on the same wavelength in stringing the details together in process of thought.

It is often reported that in the case of being bilingual in two widely differing languages, as for instance English or French on the one hand, and an African or Middle Eastern language on the other, a counterpart's thought processes actually seem to change when a switch is made from one language to the other. People with extended experience in Latin America feel that this is true even in the case of English and Spanish—that the American finds out better what his opposite **really** thinks if the conversation is conducted in Spanish. It would follow that in some situations—Japanese to English would be an example—the question for the negotiator is which pattern of thought will be the **operative** one when it comes to carrying out an agreement. Even an agreement reached with an English-speaking opposite might come to mean something quite different when it is substantially considered in the language of colleagues who do not use English.

4. As a final note, it should be kept in mind that the ability to use English or some other Western language may have an important **social status** meaning in certain areas. Despite what is heard about nationalistic pride in using the language of the local culture, people with whom Americans are most likely to do business may well feel at a disadvantage—including a social identity disadvantage—if they are not able to speak English.

In some cases, a well-meaning but inept attempt by an American to speak in the local language may even be taken as condescension. Because the ability to speak English carries a prestige value in most places, **communication difficulties can be introduced when people who speak it as a second language attempt to use it beyond their ability**. When complicated ideas and intentions are involved, the problem is greater. The American, whose ability to use the other's language is even less dependable, easily acquiesces, and in the process assumes that more accurate comprehension has been achieved than is the case.

The point to be drawn is that Americans probably fail to use interpreters when they are really needed, producing misunderstanding in more instances than one thinks. When things go wrong, the tendency is to assign negative motives rather than recognize real misunderstanding, for after all, "I distinctly said..."

In addition, the American derivation of the King's English is not the only variety. As it has become nearly a native language in places like Malaysia, India or the Philippines, local usage over time in the context of local culture has produced appreciable differences in effective meaning. The instances of inexact equivalences has increased correspondingly and has introduced communication problems in going from one English to another. In the Philippines, I have had occasion to use English-to-English interpreters for just that reason.

Finally, a thought applicable not only to this section but to the entire paper: the problem of equivalence in translation and subjective meaning is compounded when **public** interest and reaction are factors in determining the end result of negotiation for in media transmission, all the difficulties of perception and misperception are intensified. Original context is missing—new context is supplied. Only part of an intended message may be selected for transmission and then through the perceptual lens supplied by the reporter or newscaster. A far wider variety of meanings will be given to statements than was the case in the negotiation itself. The irony to be faced is that as modern technology increases the scale of communication, it does not necessarily increase its cross-cultural reliability.[25]

REFERENCES

1. John Stoessinger, **Nations in Darkness: China, Russia and America**, New York: Random House, 1971.
2. Irving Janis, **Victims of Group Think**, New York: Houghton Mifflin, 1972.
3. Robert Jervis, **Perception and Misperception in International Politics**, Princeton: Princeton Univ. Press, 1976.
4. Alexander L. George, **Presidential Decisionmaking in Foreign Policy: The Effective Use of Information and Advice**, Boulder: Westview Press, 1980.
5. Anthony Marc Lewis, "The Blind Spot of U.S. Foreign Intelligence," **Journal of Communication**, Winter, 1976, Volume 26:1, pp. 44-55.
6. Harry Triandis, a social psychologist at the University of Illinois, has been especially helpful in demonstrating the applicability of attribution theory to foreign affairs and cross-cultural communication training.
7. Role analysis in a foreign affairs setting is discussed at greater length in Glen H. Fisher, **Public Diplomacy and the Behavioral Sciences**, Bloomington: Indiana University Press, 1972. The Philippine case is reviewed as an example.
8. Raymond Vernon, "Apparatchiks and Entrepreneurs: U.S.-Soviet Economic Relations," **Foreign Affairs**, January, 1974, Volume 52, No. 2, pp. 249-262.
9. This is taken from David F. Ronfeldt and Caesar D. Sereseres, "Treating the Alien (ation) in U.S.-Mexican Relations," informal discussion paper of the Rand Corporation, 1978.

10. Glen Caudill Dealy. **The Public Man—An Interpretation of Latin American and other Catholic Countries**, Amherst: University of Massachusetts Press, 1977.

11. This was reported at some length in **The New York Times**, May 12, 1974. The author was Yoshio Terasawa.

12. Stanley Hoffman, "Perceptions, Reality, and the Franco-American Conflict," **Journal of International Affairs**, Volume XXI, 1967, No. 1, pp. 57-71.

13. Various observers have commented on the **amae** concept as a factor in the U.S.-Japanese relationship. For example, see I.M. Destler, Priscilla Clapp, Hideo Sato and Haruhiro Fukui, **Managing an Alliance: The Politics of U.S.-Japanese Relations**, Washington: The Brookings Institution, 1976, especially pp. 108-109.

14. Articulate discussion of cultural and racial factors was found in Hiroshi Kitamura, "Psychological Dimensions of U.S.-Japanese Relations," **Occasional Papers in International Affairs**, No. 28, Harvard University, Center for International Affairs, 1971.

15. See the penetrating analysis of a former high level State Department interpreter and social scientist: Edmund Glenn, **Man and Mankind: Conflict and Communication Between Cultures**, Norwood, N.J., Ablex, 1981.

16. Theodore, Zeldin, **France 1848-1945**, Vol. II (Oxford, England: Oxford University Press, 1977), p. 205.

17. For one analysis applicable to persuasion in negotiation, see E.S. Glenn, Dr. Witmeyer, and K.A. Stevenson, "Cultural Styles of Persuasion," **International Journal of Intercultural Relations**, Vol. 1, No. 3, Fall, 1977, pp. 52-66.

18. This is only superficially suggestive of differences in thought and reasoning patterns. In a more profound approach, Kinhide Mushakoji presented a paper at the Trilateral Commission Japan Seminar in May, 1975, in which he described American and Japanese styles in terms of **erabi** culture, implying the inclination to select or choose, and **awase**, implying to combine or adjust one thing to another. "The Cultural Premises of

Japanese Diplomacy," Trilateral Commission Papers, **Social and Political Issues in Japan**, 1975, pp. 17-29.

19. Edward T. Hall, **The Silent Language**, Garden City, N.Y.: Doubleday, 1959.

20. Masaaki Imai, **Never Take Yes for an Answer**, Tokyo: Simul Press, 1975.

21. Salvador de Madariaga, **Englishmen, Frenchmen, Spaniards: An Essay in Comparative Psychology**, London: Oxford University Press, 1928.

22. Lorand Szalay, Institute of Comparative and Social Studies, Inc., Washington, D.C., has developed this approach, and has applied it in various projects undertaken for government agencies concerned with cross-cultural communication analysis problems.

23. This is a specialized field of investigation. In standard journals, see Edmund S. Glenn, "Meaning and Behavior: Communication and Culture," **The Journal of Communication**, Vol. XVI, No. 4, Dec., 1966, or George A. Miller's review of **Language, Thought and Reality: Selected Writings of Benjamin Lee Whorf**, edited by John B. Carroll, in "Reconsiderations," **Human Nature**, June, 1978, Vol. 16, No. 1, pp. 92-96.

24. See especially the work of Masao Kunihiro, for example his "Indigenous Barriers to Communication," **The Japan Interpreter**, Vol. 8, No. 1, Winter, 1973, pp. 96-108.

25. For my own larger discussion of international communication relations, see Glen Fisher, **American Communication in a Global Society**, Norwood, N.J., Ablex, 1979.